Sanjay Kumar

A New H-index

Scholarly Dialogues Press

Title: A New H-index
Author: Sanjay Kumar
Publisher: Scholarly Dialogues Press, India
ISBN: 978-93-5592-389-9
ISBN: 978-93-5592-617-3 (eBook)
Edition: First
Publication Year: 2025
DOI: 10.5281/zenodo.17750583

For permissions, contact:
Email: skumarsdr@gmail.com

Category of the Book

The book will come under the following BISAC codes:

REF020000 - REFERENCE / Research
LAN004000 - LANGUAGE ARTS & DISCIPLINES/Publishing
LAN002000 - LANGUAGE ARTS & DISCIPLINES/Library & Information Science/General
EDU04000 – EDUCATION/Philosophy & Social Aspects
SCI000000 - SCIENCE/General

Preface

The present short book titled “A New H-index” is presented in the form of dialogues between two researchers. These two researchers and their dialogues are invented. The two researchers debate about the pros and cons of the h-index and its effects on various researchers. A new h-index is proposed, which is a modification of the existing h-index.

The use of imaginary dialogues is an established method for truth-seeking in science communication, pedagogy, and education. This is the first time it is applied to understand the h-index. This is written for anyone involved in scientific research or bibliometrics. The use of metaphors, humor, and narratives can make it useful also for those engaged in education and communication. It contains one chapter.

Gumla, Jharkhand, India — Sanjay Kumar

About the Author

Sanjay Kumar, Ph.D. (KUL, Belgium), did post-Ph.D. research at the following places: Utah State University (USA), National Laser Centre (South Africa), Shanghai Jiao Tong University (China), and York University (Canada). He has been active in research for the last twenty-five years (H-index 20).

He is the author of six books (publisher: Springer Cham): Additive Manufacturing Processes, 2020; Additive Manufacturing Solutions, 2021; Additive Manufacturing Classification, 2022; Additive Manufacturing Advantage, 2023; A New Theory of Additive Manufacturing, 2024: and A Concise Encyclopedia of Additive Manufacturing, 2025.

Content

Chapter 1 1
A New H-index 1
References 33
End 35

Chapter 1

A New H-index

Abstract

H-index is widely used as a metric to evaluate research output. But this metric is not free from its flaws. It is necessary to understand the pros and cons of its use and impacts. It can better be understood if two researchers start talking about it, one speaking against it and other speaking in favor of it. The present chapter shows how two imaginary researchers, R1 and R2, are talking to find a common ground. When two human beings talk, since they are not machines, they show emotions and can get irritated if one speaks against another's longstanding belief. The chapter is not free from such displays of emotions.

A new h-index is introduced, named as n-index, where "n" stands for "normalized h." It is the h-index that is calculated after dividing the citation of each paper by the number of authors of each paper. The problem with the h-index is that it is not scientific, which is given, which gives most of the problems. Thus, the n-index is free from all those problems that arise due to the unscientific nature of the h-index. Therefore, it is claimed that the n-index is better than the h-index, but it is not claimed that the n-index is the solution to all problems.

Kumar, S. (2025). *A New H index*. Scholarly Dialogues Press.
ISBN: 978-93-5592-389-9

Conversations

Researcher named **R1:** Do you want to change the h-index [1-2]?

Researcher named **R2:**. Yes.

R1: You are not the only one who wants to change it [3]. But why?

R2: Because people complain about it [4-6].

R1: What are their complaints?

R2: Senior researchers complain that the methods used in the h-index do not help represent their true output.

R1: How?

R2: They collaborate with many research groups, and they publish papers bearing all the names of the collaborators. But there are other researchers who do not collaborate and publish papers bearing the names of many people, creating confusion and undermining the research collaboration.

R1: If other researchers do not collaborate, how will their paper bear the names of many people?

R2: It is by increasing the number of authors by manipulation [7].

R1: How does it affect senior researchers?

R2: The method used in the h-index does not take into account the reason for authorship. Therefore, the h-index is not affected by the reason for an increase in the number of authors. It means if the number is increased by collaboration or manipulation, the result is the same. Thus, the h-index does not distinguish between a large and a small research group. If the method were able to capture manipulation of authorship, the method would have been fair.

R1: I want to laugh at your logic. I have always heard that senior researchers are the main beneficiaries of the method used in the h-index. These are they who have accumulated citations and h-index over years; these are they who have a high number of citations and h-index. Therefore, their h-index should be calculated with respect to their years of work [8-9]. Why will they complain?

R2: They are not complaining because they have high a h-index and citations; they are complaining because others have also got h-indices and citations by manipulation.

R1: Is it possible to distinguish and check such malpractice?

R2: It is indirectly possible.

R1: How?

R2: By changing the h-index?

R1: What is the problem in it?

R2: It is unscientific. This is the root cause of all problems.

R1: What is unscientific here?

R2: Science says nothing comes out of the blue – either it is created or converted. For example, electricity will not come to your home unless someone supplies electricity to your home. Electricity is created somewhere and then supplied. If the electric company disconnects the supply, electricity will not reach your home even if you use a robust wire to transport the electricity. If someone says electricity will come to your home if you use a shining wire, even if the electric company disconnects, it is unscientific. Because the wire does not create electricity, it is only a means to transport. If there is no source of electricity, the electricity should not be felt anywhere.

When some publication cites your paper, your paper gets one citation. If many publications cite your paper, your paper gets many citations. The number of citations garnered by your paper depends upon how many publications cited your paper. The moment someone says the number of citations your paper gets will depend not only on the number of citations but also on how citations are reported – it is unscientific. The h-index uses a methodology that works like a shining wire to supply citations in the absence of the source of citations.

R1: Do you want to say the h-index uses a wrong method to report citations?

R2: Yes. The h-index inflates one's output. As the h-index depends on the number of citations, and the number of citations is inflated, the h-index is inflated.

R1: How?

R2: If one person publishes one paper and his paper gets ten citations, he has only ten citations from his paper. If ten persons publish one paper and the paper gets ten citations. Each of the ten persons is entitled to claim ten citations from the same paper. Thus, the total citation that comes from the same paper is ten multiplied by ten, i.e., one hundred. Thus, ten citations are inflated to a hundred citations. It means ten citations become one hundred citations when the number of authors increases from one to ten. The paper got only ten citations, but it generated 90 more citations out of nothing.

R1: Can you say, in a nutshell, what this numbering of citations conveys?

R2: It conveys that if you go to a supermarket named H-index, the gatekeeper of the supermarket asks two questions: 1) How much money do you have? and 2) How many of you are coming today? If your answer is that you have ten dollars and you are alone. The gatekeeper will say, "In our supermarket you can buy goods equivalent to ten dollars." If your answer is that you have ten dollars and you have ten people along with you. The gatekeeper will say, "In our supermarket, you can buy goods equivalent to a hundred dollars."

R1: I have never heard of such a supermarket. If I go to a supermarket, my money always remains the same irrespective of the persons I take along with me. Why is H-index supermarket such that?

R2: Whenever it sees many people, it becomes happy and gives discounts.

R1: Anyway. How are each of the ten persons entitled to claim ten citations from the same paper?

R2: For example, when each of the ten persons creates a Google Scholar profile [10], ten citations are added to each profile. The total citation of each person increases by ten. Henceforth, they can claim they have ten more citations.

R1: How does it affect the h-index?

R2: The first person who publishes one paper gets an h-index of one [11]; the first person has given a one hundred percent contribution. Each one of the ten persons from the second paper also gets an h-index of one, while each one has only one-tenth of the contribution [12]. Is it not unfair to the first person?

R1: No.

R2: Why?

R1: Both papers are different. Their qualities are different. If ten persons make one paper, it means there is a research collaboration. The paper shows that ten persons have contributed to make the paper. If they had not contributed, the paper would not have been made. Giving one h-index to each person shows that their contributions should be celebrated and they should be rewarded even if the paper shows that each has only one-tenth of the contribution.

R2: Is it fair to the first person?

R1: Why did the first person publish alone? It shows that the first person is not fit to collaborate. Research work is a collaborative work. Therefore, even if there are multiple authors in one paper, all are entitled to be given one h-index instead of one-tenth of an h-index.

R2: Do you want all persons who are publishing alone to not publish alone? Do you not want to see a person being alone? Are you running a marriage bureau? Do you want all small research groups to become large research groups? Do you not like a small research group? Are you the director of a funding agency that has a lot of free money to distribute to avoid tax? A paper that has ten authors does not necessarily show that the paper is due to a research collaboration.

R1: If they did not do collaboration, what did they do? Can you give any examples?

R2: If one person publishes one paper and gets ten citations, he has ten citations and one h-index. If there are nine persons, each of whom publishes one paper and gets ten citations, each person will get ten citations and one h-index. If these ten persons are not happy with their h-index and want to improve their h-index without writing any more papers, they need to come together. If these ten persons come together and give authorship to each other, there will be ten papers having ten authors each. If each paper gets ten citations, each person will be having 100 citations and a 10 h-index. These people came together for an adjustment of authorship to increase their h-index ten times. Is this fair?

R1: This is what a senior researcher was complaining about. People can increase their h-index by manipulation or adjustment of authorship. But how will they be able to publish it?

R2: What is the problem?

R1: They need to declare who did what before an editor accepts it.

R2: They will declare that the first author made the first draft, the 2nd author made the 2nd draft, and so on. How will the editor know who did what? The editor will not verify by calling the head of the department or institution. The editor does not ask them to submit an affidavit signed in the presence of a magistrate or a notary. The editor will not visit the lab personally to check what they are doing. The editor also cannot employ a private detective agency to find the truth. The editor is helpless.

R1: You are underestimating an editor. Editors are those who have already published a lot of papers; that is why they became editors. They have a developed sense of intuition and can guess when the authors are lying.

R2: Then, why did editors ask authors to declare who did what?

R1: It is to fulfil the formality.

R2: What is the basis for the formality?

R1: To make sure that authors are morally bound. The system relies on the conscience of authors. It is expected that authors are upright.

R2: What will an editor do if authors are not upright?

R1: Editors are powerful; they can withdraw the paper after publication. They always do it whenever they are informed about the malpractice.

R2: Do you want editors to first publish a paper and then withdraw it?

R1: I do not want that, but editors are powerful.

R2: Who will inform them about the malpractice?

R1: Readers, authors, other editors, and "well-wishers" of those authors.

R2: It means editors depend on others to check the malpractice.

R1: Yes

R2: Is not this dependency a helplessness?

R1: If you derive this meaning, then you can say so.

R2: How can an editor be made more powerful so they will not be so helpless to depend on others?

R1: I do not know. They need to depend, because of a few special authors.

R2: Why do these special authors submit to publish?

R1: I do not want to talk about those who engage in malpractice. They need to be banned.

R2: Are they not part of society?

R1: It seems you have more sympathy for them.

R2: Is not society responsible for what they do?

R1: How can society be responsible for the actions of these people? These people want a shortcut to success. These people do not want to do hard work. Whether society has asked them not to do hard work?

R2: Why are they not motivated to do hard work?

R1: Some people are like this. Whatever you do, they will not change.

R2: How can you generalize?

R1: I am not generalizing. You are generalizing by blindly supporting those who engage in malpractice.

R2: I am not supporting all. But do you want to understand why some of them do?

R1: Why do they do?

R2: Because they are forced to do that.

R1: How?

R2: When you mean research collaboration by adjustment of authorship, they do adjustment of authorship to prove that you are right.

R1: When they do adjustment of authorship instead of doing research collaboration, how are they right?

R2: Who made them wrong?

R1: How did anyone make them wrong?

R2: If you do not have the means to distinguish between a research collaboration and an adjustment of authorship, who has given you the right to equate a research collaboration with the number of authors?

R1: How is anyone equating them?

R2: By supporting the h-index.

R1: Do you think the h-index is a problem? All scholars use it. Everywhere, it is used as a benchmark for research evaluation. It is one of the criteria to get various jobs. If it were a problem, why had so many people been using it? Do you think the h-index motivates someone to commit crime?

R2: Yes.

R1: Please explain.

R2: When the h-index rewards multi-author publication without knowing the source of multi-authorship. The h-index motivates scholars to convert their publications from having few authors to many authors. The motivation could be due to the intention to encourage the collaboration. But if the h-index does not have the means to verify collaboration, the h-index cannot be free from encouraging artificial multi-authorship. If an author submits such a multi-author paper to a journal by unjust declaration, where is he getting motivation from? The author commits a crime that cannot be easily checked by an editor. He is doing it because the h-index refuses to give him his due. By depriving the author of his right, the h-index is forcing the author to become a criminal. No one wants to see why he commits crime; all want to see what his crime is. Who is the real criminal out of the two: the one who commits or the one who motivates to commit?

R1: You are exaggerating. The h-index is used by most scholars and is known to almost everyone. If a person applies for jobs, positions, or grants, their h-index goes through scrutiny with the help of the library. The scrutiny will show who the person is irrespective of their h-index. If there are some papers that have many authors, one's contribution can be checked by knowing the position of one's name among the authors. If someone is the first author, it is valuable. If someone's name always comes at the 4th or 5th position, one will not be appreciated even if one has a high h-index. Similarly, if someone has some papers having only one or two authors, those papers will stand out even if one has a low h-index. H-index is not the only criterion that is used to evaluate [13]. Reference checks, plans from the candidates, interviews, background checks, etc. are used, which will not allow a skewed h-index to dominate. What you are saying is exaggerating the importance of the h-index, and then exaggerating its effect on the publication behaviour of a person. As per you, the h-index is the root cause of all evils in our society, and the moment the h-index disappears, all problems in our society will disappear.

R2: This is how you want a problem to be solved. As per you, the importance of the problem should be decreased. It should be consistently decreased, so after some time, the problem will look smaller. As the problem will look smaller or insignificant, then what is the need to ponder over it? First you said the multi-author publication always represents a research collaboration. Now, you are saying even if it affects the h-index, there is no need to worry. Because there are other measures, such as reference checks, already in place to mitigate the effect. Therefore, there exists no problem. Is this what you want to say?

R1: As I said earlier, you are exaggerating. You want to say that all researchers dream about the h-index all the time. Therefore, the moment they find that there is a scope for adjustment of authorship, they go forward and do the adjustment so that their h-index will increase. You are ignoring a number of other reasons why the authorship of a paper does not always represent the rightful owner of the paper. For example, it can happen in exchange for a favour, or to give respect to other colleagues who have not directly contributed but have created an infrastructure that enabled the research work to happen. It can also happen when a researcher has sympathy for one's colleague who needs authorship for promotion or for the extension of employment. It can also happen as a prelude to applying for a grant, when the co-authorship is required to justify that the collaboration will not be new but will be the continuation of their past works. It can also happen when one person wants employment and the other wants authorship. It can again happen when a junior researcher wants to increase the visibility of his paper and requests a senior and famous researcher to become co-author so his paper will get more attention. Thus, you can see there are various reasons why the number of authors increases. Please say where the h-index is present among these reasons to motivate a person to commit crime. Are you not downplaying the role of other reasons?

R2: At least, you have accepted that h-index is one of many reasons. And since there are many reasons, the role of the h-index is very small. Is this?

R1: Again, you are making something out of nothing. In the beginning, it was the senior researcher who was complaining about the manipulation of authorship. Just now, it is the junior researcher who is manipulating the authorship to increase the h-index, because the h-index is unfair to him. A senior researcher is a victim because of junior researchers. A junior researcher is also a victim because of senior researchers. Just tell me, who is the victim?

R2: Both are victims.

R1: What is the solution?

R2: Divide the number of citations of a paper by the number of authors of that paper. It will normalise the number of citations and then the h-index. The new h-index that will come will be better. You can call it n-index. "N" stands for "normalised h."

R1: Normalising is not new [14]. Can you give an example of how it works?

R2: For example, there are three co-authors of a paper. They publish nine papers, and each paper gets nine citations. Each of the authors will have an h-index of 9 and 81 citations. If you divide the number of citations of each paper by three authors. Each paper will have three citations, and the total citations will be 27. Thus, each author will have an n-index of 3 and 27 citations.

R1: What will happen if one of the papers gets just one citation?

R2: Then, their h-index will be 8 and total citations will be 73, while their n-index will still be 3 and total citations will be 24.33.

R1: So, their total citations can end up as a fractional number.

R2: Yes.

R1: Whether people will be happy with fractional citations?

R2: They should be happy because it shows their true identity.

R1: What if the people are not happy?

R2: If they are not happy, it means they are not happy with their true identity.

R1: I want to laugh and laugh at your solution.

R2: Why?

R1: People use the h-index because it inflates their output. If the h-index is normalised, the h-index of most of the people will decrease drastically. Then, people will not like to mention it. Their scholar profiles will disappear. For example, if Google Scholar profiles start to disappear, citations of related papers start to decrease. If citations from papers decrease, a decreased number of papers will be submitted to Google Scholar. If a decreased number of papers will be submitted, citations of existing papers will further decrease. If papers start disappearing from Google Scholar, scholars will stop visiting Google Scholar. If few people visit the site, the importance of the site will decrease. Another Google-type site will arise with new features, and people will start shifting to the new site. Therefore, the h-index is not a problem. Willingness to reject the h-index is a problem. For example, someone will not like to have their h-index decreased from 100 to 30 and total citations decreased from 20,000 to 5,000. The h-index is present because most researchers like it.

R2: It is my time to laugh and laugh at your prediction. Do you want to say when the dollar will be devalued, only my money will decrease? If the h-index and citations are decreased, everyone's h-index and citations will decrease. Is it not when a big h-index will become a small h-index, a small h-index will look like a big one? There will be some exceptions. But which one is better: some exceptions or mass victimization?

R1: I am so sorry that I could not explain why most researchers like it. Can I explain?.

R2: Please go ahead.

R1: Most of the researchers like it or have nothing to say against it because most of them think that they are getting less than what they deserve. If you ask an assistant professor whether he is getting what he deserves, he will say, "I deserve to be a senior professor; I know many senior professors who have less output than me." If you ask the same question to an associate professor, he will reply, "Being an assistant professor was better; I can neither quit nor wait." If you ask a Ph.D. student, he will reply, "My output is more than the combined output of two Ph.D. students of a nearby lab, and I am still asked to do more for my Ph.D." If you ask a master student, he will reply, "I don't know why I have not got an excellent grade in the project work. My project is the original project. I don't think anyone in our department knows more than me about this project." If you ask a senior professor, he will reply, "It is already too late; I had to be given the most prestigious award thirty years back. Even my students are getting all sorts of awards these days. If it does not happen soon, then, one day, my students will be in the committee to decide whether I should be given the award." If you make any more mistakes by asking them to justify their output, then please be assured that they will consume your whole day, and even then the listing of their achievements will not finish. Most of the researchers, in a sense, are victims.

R2: How is this related to the h-index?

R1: When a researcher feels that he is getting less than what he deserves, he does not see the inflation of his output as an inflation but as a token to compensate for his loss. For him, the methodology used to calculate the h-index is not inflating his output but is unable to show his true output. He has different sorts of complaints. He has published some papers in high-impact journals. Why is h-index method not able to distinguish his star papers from the conference papers of other researchers? Why is the h-index method not taking extra measures to further inflate the citation of these star papers? According to him, his star paper is equal to ten conference papers of other researchers. He has more complaints. One of his papers has got two thousand citations, while his h-index is 35. He is complaining about why this paper is not getting extra consideration. Why is the h-index method not able to reward him extra for this groundbreaking work? Why should not his paper of two thousand citations be considered equivalent to 20 papers of 100 citations each? If it will be considered so, his h-index has a chance to increase from 35 to 55. According to him, the h-index method is doing injustice to him by deflating his h-index. Do you accept his paper as groundbreaking?

R2: Yes. It is the number of citations that distinguishes a groundbreaking paper from an ordinary paper. If authors want to make their paper groundbreaking by self-citations [15], it is not possible. Because then, they have to publish many papers on the similar topic and then go through the infamy of committing self-citations. If they do, they will increase the citation of their paper by some hundred but not by some thousand. Thus, other publications need to cite that paper in large numbers [16]. Therefore, the number of citations to equate the groundbreaking is not illogical. It is possible that some paper is groundbreaking but is not getting many citations because the field is new and many people are not working. In this case as well, if the paper is groundbreaking, it will get relatively more citations than other papers in the same new field.

R1: Then, is it fair if his groundbreaking paper is not given extra consideration for calculating his h-index?

R2: The increased citation is already reflected in the total citation. What other things does he want?

R1: His citation from the groundbreaking paper should be distributed among other papers, so his h-index will increase.

R2: Will it not further inflate his output?

R1: Is not distributing citations among other papers deflating his output? Why are you not considering the hard work he did to make a paper a groundbreaking paper?

R2: The hard work he did was his conscious decision. He was aware that he could write many conference papers with the same hard work. But, instead, he chose to do hard work, for which he was already rewarded with more citations. Did the method in the h-index reduce the citation of his groundbreaking paper to calculate the total citation? What will happen if his groundbreaking paper is removed considering it an outlier? Does it not happen in making curves, when we remove those data that show extreme value? Therefore, those papers that have very high citations should be removed?

R1: How can you be so cruel to him?

R2: He is not understanding the basic thing. Once you have spent your money to eat an expensive meal, you cannot repent and say, "My money should be returned because it was a huge amount of money. I want to spend that money to eat frozen pizza for many days instead of just one expensive meal." If he did the hard work, he got knowledge and wisdom. He should cherish it. If he spent the money on the expensive meal, he should also cherish those candlelight moments, those selfies taken in dim light, those silent talks with hanging artworks, and those king-like moments. If he is repenting so much for why he spent his hard-earned money on such an expensive meal, he is advised to eat frozen pizza for the rest of his life. My advice is simple: "If you want to have an expensive dinner next time, then please make sure that you do it only in your dream." I mean, he should not invest his hard work in making any more groundbreaking papers and look only for conference proceedings to submit.

R1: Do you not have any sympathy for his cause?

R2: His demand is illogical. His demand is based on a premise that he will never have all his papers be groundbreaking. It is a pessimistic view. What will happen if all of his papers are groundbreaking? Then, citations from which paper will be transferred to which paper? If he has twenty papers, and all twenty papers have 2000 citations. How can his h-index further increase by distribution? Then, his demand will be that each paper should be considered equal to twenty papers based on the citations they got? Then, what will his h-index give impression? He will be having an h-index of more than 200 from 20 papers. Will it not confuse people about the number of his papers?

R1: What a contradiction! Now, you are supporting the h-index. In the beginning, you were finding faults in the h-index. Why do you not show some consistency?

R2: I am not supporting the h-index. I am only opposing the unfair demands of that person. If you want to infer that since I am opposing that person, I am standing along with the h-index, then I cannot help. Let me clarify that the methods used in the h-index are the root cause of his demands.

R1: How?

R2: When the h-index inflates the output, the genuine reason that should inflate the output is not pronounced. If the contribution due to his groundbreaking work is not prominent, it is because his output is already inflated due to some other papers. It has nothing to do with him; it has only to do with the method used in the h-index. His grievances come due to the wrong method. If there were no such method, there would not have been such grievances.

R1: His demand is not illogical. You are missing the point. The h-index carries more prestige, while total citation carries less prestige. It is preferable to have a high h-index plus low total citation than a low h-index and high total citation. Because a high h-index immediately conveys the presence of prestigious papers, while a high total citation does not have such conveying power. A combination of low h-index and high total citation intends to confuse and can invite unwanted scrutiny. A groundbreaking paper means prestige. And if this prestige is not allowed to improve the h-index, the resulting h-index fails to show the true prestige of the author.

R2: The total citation is not as respectable as the h-index, because the methods used in the h-index generates citations, as I said earlier. That is why the n-index is proposed. Here, there is no unwarranted citation, and therefore, each citation counts. And the transfer of citations is not required to earn the required prestige.

R1: Are you not aware of the g-index [17]?

R2: What is it?

R1: If you do not know, there is no benefit in informing you. Just let me tell you that it takes into account the citations earned by such groundbreaking papers.

R2: Please explain.

R1: Citations from all papers are added, so the citations from all papers are counted. The square root of the total citation is calculated. This is the g-index. For example, if the total citation is 81, 9 is the square root of 81. The g-index is 9 if the author has at least 9 papers.

R2: What if one paper has 81 citations and each of the other papers has 0 citations?

R1: Even then, the g-index is 9. This is how importance to a groundbreaking paper is given.

R2: Then, what is his h-index?

R1: His h-index is 1.

R2: G-index is 9 and h-index is 1! Then, it is easier to get a higher g-index than an h-index.

R1: Yes, the g-index is always more than the h-index.

R2: It means if the h-index inflates the output, the g-index hyperinflates it. Besides, it misleads.

R1: How does it mislead?

R2: For getting an h-index of 9, each paper should have 9 citations. For getting a g-index of 9, if the citation of any paper is small, there is no need to worry because other papers are there to compensate. It means just make one groundbreaking paper and take rest, the rest of your life. Have just one good paper, and submit all other papers to conferences. This is what you want all researchers to have direction.

R1: A citation is just like a dollar. What does it matter from which source I earn, as long as I earn legitimately? After all, whatever I earn, comes to my household. When I do not earn from some source, I do not complain. Then, when I earn well from some source, why shall I not be allowed to celebrate? Why should there be any discrimination based on from which source I earn? When my paper got fewer citations, I did not ask to have more index. But when my paper got excellent citations, why should I be deprived of more index?

R2: I remember my school days. I used to get more marks, almost 100 percent, in literature. But I was not good at mathematics and science and used to fail in these two subjects. Since these two subjects were compulsory, I used to fail in the class even though I earned good marks in the literature. I left the school and started fishing. My parents wanted me to be educated. They were rich. They got me admitted to an expensive school, and I never failed. Because the school had a rule that all marks should be combined and the average should be calculated. If the average mark is more than the passing mark of any subject, the students will always pass. The result is that I ended up becoming a novelist, and I am still not able to calculate accurately how much I earn from my novels.

R1: What do you want to say?

R2: Getting minimum marks in compulsory subjects was necessary for the all-round development of students. It was necessary to maintain the quality of students and the quality of education. For getting a certain g-index, there is no minimum number of citations required for a paper. Since citation is associated with quality. The g-index is not able to show the quality of a researcher. It does not inform whether a certain g-index corresponds to a certain quality of papers. While the H-index shows the quality, because of getting a certain h-index, one needs to have certain papers having a certain citation. This minimum threshold does not exist in the g-index. The g-index is not able to abstract certain objective information from a list of publications and total citations. Since it does not give a clear indication of the quality of a researcher, people will preferably ask for a list of publications and total citations instead of the g-index of a person. It does not make sense to remove the minimum threshold. If excess citation looks problematic, then there can be another measure for it, but not at the cost of the threshold [18-19].

R1: Why not use both indices [20]?

R2: We are looking for one, not many.

R1: Do you want to say the quality of a paper is equal to the citation of a paper?

R2: Yes, it is. How does a metric work if it does not equate the quality of a paper with the number of its citations?

R1: What about review papers? A review paper generally gets more citations than a research paper. Do you want to say a research paper has less quality than a review paper?

R2: The debate associated with a review paper and a research paper has been happening for a long time and will continue as long as this universe lasts.

R1: Why do you say so?

R2: Do you want to say a review paper has come from Mars and a research paper has come from Venus? Are they not the different faces of the same coin? Who writes a review paper? Only a researcher who can write a good research paper. Who writes a research paper – only a researcher, who knows the field in and out, can write an authoritative review paper. Do you know a rcscarch paper that does not contain the section Introduction? What is Introduction? Is Introduction not a prelude for a review paper? Without reviewing many articles, how can a researcher write Introduction? If he can review many articles, why can he not write a review paper? Thus, a researcher can write a review paper if he is willing to write. If he is aware that a review paper gives more citations, why does he not want to write it? A review paper gets more citations because it serves many researchers. Does he not want to sacrifice his research to serve other researchers?

R1: What if he sacrifices his research time and writes both research and review papers? Will he get more citations for his research paper than his review paper? If a metric is for quality, as you already mentioned, why should the value of the metric or index increase for his service rather than the quality of his research?

R2: If a person writes both research and review papers, and he gets fewer citations in his research paper than his review paper, then the quality of his research is not good. How does he define new research? He might have changed some parameters or conditions, or some little new information, and got his 'research' paper published. A good research paper becomes a seminal paper that defines a generation. Do you know a review paper that ever became a seminal paper? If a good research paper is not getting citations, it means it is taking time to accumulate citations [21]. You are not supposed to check citations after some months and give your judgement.

R1: What about those people that have made industries out of writing small review papers? They are those who are getting mostly benefited by research metrics. They write a number of small review papers without writing any research papers, and they improve both their h-index and total citation.

R2: I am talking only about an authoritative review paper that only a researcher can write. If someone is writing a review paper of other fields than his research field, the review paper will get more citations than a research paper, but only in the beginning. That type of review paper does not get more than 50 citations unless the field is biology or nanoscience.

R1: After all, he got 50 citations from a shallow review paper. I got only 20 citations from one of my good research papers. Is it fair to me? The h-index says that I have less quality than a shallow review-paper writer. Do you agree with the quality shown by the h-index? I mean, do you agree with the quality shown by your n-index, as the n-index like the h-index is also silent on this issue?

R2: I do not agree with you that the n-index is silent on this issue. You cannot equate the n-index with the h-index as far as this issue is concerned. Let us pause for a moment and check where those review papers come from. The people who publish a number of small review papers do not do it alone. They are a group of people. The n-index directly addresses this issue when its methodology divides the citation by the number of authors. This methodology breaks the group; it does not reward the group activity as a group enterprise. It gives an impression why to become partners in crime, because all will be taken to task individually.

R1: Do you want to say a researcher does not write alone an unauthoritative review paper and increase the citation? How does the n-index check it?

R2: The n-index does not check it, nor does it want to check it. Actually, the n-index encourages a person to engage in writing and gain knowledge even if the subject is different, if the person is willing to invest their time. If a group activity is not rewarded, more individuals will come forward to write review papers because the citation earned from their review papers will become more prominent in the presence of a general decrease in the total citation if the n-index is adopted.

R1: You are twisting my concern. I am sorry that I am not able to say what I wanted to say. I am not against an individual getting citations by his hard work. I want to say that citations are increased by unfair means; how can it be checked?

R2: Please specify what unfair means is? Please give an example.

R1: These are open access publications. These are new trends these days. Just give money, and your paper will become an OA publication.

R2: What is wrong with it?

R1: I am working in a lab that does not have many resources. When I submit my papers to a journal, they ask me whether I want to have OA publication. I always say no, because our lab does not have the funds to support it. If my paper were OA, many people would have accessed it, and my paper would have had more chance to get more citations. It is a known fact that OA papers get more citations than papers of equivalent quality that are not OA. Is it not fair to me that I am getting fewer citations because I do not have funds? Is not giving money for OA the same as giving a bribe to get more citations?

R2: You are submitting a paper. So you are in a better position than many people who are not in a position to submit as well. Because they do not have resources to reach your stage. When your paper is published, your paper will be in a queue to get citations and be counted for your h-index. Is it not discrimination against those people? Why should these people not be given some discount in h-index so that if they get an h-index of 10, they should be given 20 percent more h-index, so their h-index will become 12? Do you not have sympathy for these people?

R1: How is it related to my question on OA?

R2: Because of OA, many people have access to some resources. If you go to Google and search these days, you will find many publications because of OA. Do you remember how the situation was there some years back?

R1: I understand the benefit of OA. I am not against it; I myself am a beneficiary of it. I support it.

R2: How are you supporting it if you do not see the bigger picture?

R1: My question is why I should be compared with poor people. Why should I not be compared with rich people?

R2: My question is why rich people should be compared with you if you do not want to be compared with poor people.

R1: So, do you justify that I should have fewer citations because I do not have money to pay for OA?

R2: Just tell me, what is your expectation from a research metric or an index? Do you want it to be made such a robust one that it will retroactively solve all the problems of the society? Do you want it to solve all problems associated with research? A research metric is just to see the citations and make a meaning out of them. If there is some major problem, that can be considered. The n-index is proposed because there was some major problem, but it does not mean it is the solution to all ills.

R1: Do you want to say there are many ills, and OA is one of those ills for which there are no solutions offered by a research metric?

R2: OA is not one of the ills but is one of the solutions. But it can be a matter of discussion why a weightage system should not be introduced to give different weights to different papers.

R1: Do you think it will work?

R2: To some extent.

R1: Why?

R2: For example, a paper published in a high-impact journal will be given some extra weightage, so if its paper gets one citation, it becomes 1.2 citations, because it got 20 percent more weight. Then, this high-impact journal will become a higher-impact journal.

R1: Why?

R2: A journal has a high impact factor because it is cited more [22]. If you give more weightage to its citation, then its impact factor will again increase. Then the situation will become just like a rich person becoming richer and a poor person becoming poorer.

R1: Why not less weightage should be given to OA papers and review papers?

R2: Then why will people pay for having OA? Then, we are going backward when few people had resources. If there is less weightage to a review paper, why will people write it? If there will be no review paper, how will new researchers start their research, or how will researchers know other fields conveniently?

R1: If a research paper gets fewer citations, why will people write research papers?

R2: A researcher writes a research paper because it is his primary output. Writing a research paper comes under his duty. Without research papers, a person will not get a Ph.D. Without research papers, a professor will not get a grant or job or will not get a promotion. Research papers are the primary requirement of a funding agency. Before giving grants, a funding agency asks how you have advanced the knowledge or how you will advance knowledge by utilising the fund you have requested. The moment you tell them that you will advance knowledge by writing review papers. You will not get any funds.

R1: Does it mean that writing review papers is not advancing the knowledge?

R2: A review paper is not considered a primary research output. It synthesizes other works and advances the knowledge. But it does not advance the knowledge by working in lab-based research, by doing experiments, by developing equations for modelling and validating the models by using software, or by generating data to be used in a model. A review paper is just like finding out what your neighbours are doing, while a research paper is like saying what you are doing. A researcher will survive without writing review papers but will not survive without writing research papers.

R1: Then, why will people write review papers?

R2: To get citations.

R1: Is it not wrong?

R2: Is it right to have no review papers?

R1: If review papers are required, then why is it not called a primary research output?

R2: Because it is not a primary research output. It is a service. It is generally considered a service, but it is not explicitly classified as a service because most researchers will then know that it is a service and will not write review papers.

R1: Do you want to say that most people write review papers out of ignorance?

R2: Many people write it because they cannot write research papers.

R1: You are confusing me. Which one is more difficult to write: a research paper or a review paper?

R2: For those who write research papers, for them writing a review paper is relatively difficult because they have to break their rhythm of writing research papers and then have to look at what their neighbours are doing and have done. For those who write serial review papers, writing a research paper is difficult because then they have to break their rhythm of writing; they have to break their rhythm of looking only in their neighbourhood. They need to walk to their labs. They need to update their software. It might have been a long time since they last coded. Difficulty comes from the mindset.

R1: What you say does not solve the problem of citations. Do you want to say that each citation got by whatever means represents quality?

R2: Each citation does not represent quality. But each citation should be considered to represent quality when citation-based research metrics is considered to evaluate the research output.

R1: Why?

R2: If you want to evaluate research output depending on the citation, then you should have respect and acceptance for the citation. It is just like that you want to drink winc and do not like to have alcohol in it because the alcohol deteriorates your health. It is just like you want candy and do not want to have sugar in it because you are concerned about diabetes. Alcohol is an essential part of wine. Sugar is an essential part of candy. And you doubt each and every citation the moment you come near a citation-based metric.

R1: Let us have coffee.

References

1. Bornmann, L., & Daniel, H. D. (2007). What do we know about the h index? *Journal of the American*

Society for Information Science and technology, *58*(9), 1381-1385.

2. Hirsch, J. E., & Buela-Casal, G. (2014). The meaning of the h-index. *International Journal of Clinical and Health Psychology*, *14*(2), 161-164.
3. Bihari, A., Tripathi, S., & Deepak, A. (2023). A review on h-index and its alternative indices. *Journal of Information Science*, *49*(3), 624-665.
4. Bornmann, L., & Daniel, H. D. (2005). Does the h-index for ranking of scientists really work? *Scientometrics*, *65*(3), 391-392.
5. Glänzel, W. (2006). On the opportunities and limitations of the H-index. *Science focus*, *1*(1), 10-11.
6. Waltman, L., & Van Eck, N. J. (2012). The inconsistency of the h-index. *Journal of the American Society for Information Science and Technology*, *63*(2), 406-415.
7. Poirrier, M., Moreno, S., & Huerta-Cánepa, G. (2021). Robust h-index. *Scientometrics*, *126*(3), 1969-1981.
8. Kelly, C. D., & Jennions, M. D. (2006). The h index and career assessment by numbers. *Trends in Ecology & Evolution*, *21*(4), 167-170.
9. Jin, B., Liang, L., Rousseau, R., & Egghe, L. (2007). The R-and AR-indices: Complementing the h-index. *Chinese science bulletin*, *52*(6), 855-863.
10. Mondal, H., Deepak, K. K., Gupta, M., & Kumar, R. (2023). The h-Index: Understanding its predictors, significance, and criticism. *Journal of Family Medicine and Primary Care*, *12*(11), 2531-2537.
11. Bornmann, L., & Daniel, H. D. (2009). The state of h index research: Is the h index the ideal way to measure research performance? *EMBO reports*, *10*(1), 2-6.
12. Koltun, V., & Hafner, D. (2021). The h-index is no longer an effective correlate of scientific reputation. *PLoS One*, *16*(6), e0253397.
13. Khan, N. R., Thompson, C. J., Taylor, D. R., et al (2013). Part II: Should the h-index be modified? An analysis of the m-quotient, contemporary h-index, authorship value, and impact factor. *World neurosurgery*, *80*(6), 766-774.

14. Schreiber, M. (2008). A modification of the h-index: The hm-index accounts for multi-authored manuscripts. *Journal of Informetrics*, *2*(3), 211-216.
15. Engqvist, L., & Frommen, J. G. (2008). The h-index and self-citations. *Proc. Natl. Acad. Sci. USA*, *99*, 11270-11274.
16. Bartneck, C., & Kokkelmans, S. (2011). Detecting h-index manipulation through self-citation analysis. *Scientometrics*, *87*(1), 85-98.
17. Egghe, L. (2006). An improvement of the h-index: The g-index. ISSI.
18. Zhang, C. T. (2009). The e-index, complementing the h-index for excess citations. *PloS one*, *4*(5), e5429.
19. Zhang, C. T. (2013). The h'-index, effectively improving the h-index based on the citation distribution. *PloS one*, *8*(4), e59912.
20. Costas, R., & Bordons, M. (2008). Is g-index better than h-index? An exploratory study at the individual level. *Scientometrics*, *77*(2), 267-288.
21. Hirsch, J. E., & Buela-Casal, G. (2014). The meaning of the h-index. *International Journal of Clinical and Health Psychology*, *14*(2), 161-164.
22. Hodge, D. R., & Lacasse, J. R. (2011). Evaluating journal quality: Is the H-index a better measure than impact factors? *Research on Social Work Practice*, *21*(2), 222-230.

End

www.ingramcontent.com/pod-product-compliance
Ingram Content Group UK Ltd.
Pitfield, Milton Keynes, MK11 3LW, UK
UKHW021410190726
13845UKWH00028B/1008

9 789355 923899